Paddy Wailey-Hammett

Europe's New York:
Downtown Liverpool

Co Loa Media

Europe's New York:
Downtown Liverpool

Paddy Wailey-Hammett was born in Liverpool in 1995. He played for Southport and Chester FC youth teams. He works now as a Personal Trainer and a Deliveroo Delivery Driver. He got the idea for this project when his scooter was nearly robbed on the outskirts of the City and he realised he did not know half of its districts even though he travelled through them every day. The book is an introduction to a project which will stretch from Liverpool One to Thirty Eight.

Europe's New York:
Downtown Liverpool

Paddy Wailey-Hammett

Co loa Books

Co Loa Media

First published 2021 by Co loa Books
Co loa Media
Cheltenham
GLOS
GL52 2DA

Layout by Daniel Turner

ISBN 978 0 9928962 8 7

For Alex O'Reilly

Acknowledgements

To Ian Morris, Kenny Merhtens, John Hollingsworth and Andy Savery at Co Loa who have all helped me with this book.

Introduction

Liverpool is a city of constant movement, a place that never stands still. Football, Boxing and Music are lived and breathed here as well as our love for a party or anything else that involves rhythm whether that be a kid doing a wheelie, an old man rowing a kayak on the Mersey or a granny kicking her heels up at Garlands. Liverpool's movement comes in many different forms and travels as far as fashion. New and unique and often absent to a foreign eye, styles are created and move with time, a theme that is blatant amongst brackets of the younger generation of Liverpudlians who unintentionally set trends for neighbouring towns and cities with looks as abstract as a 60s style mop of uncombed hair, brandished as a 'ket wig', a craze that would undoubtedly grant a smile from The Beatles.

Liverpool's individuality can be traced centuries to when all sorts of wanderers washed up on its shores. Its spirit was most apparent during the 'Thatcher Years' when, like the Second World War, the city took a terrible battering but didn't go under. The will to stand up and walk our own path in contrast to being switched on and off like a tap infuriates many ingrates with their love for the Queen and hatred of any cosmopolitan view other than an inward looking Brexit.

Liverpool is island within England, not in a geographical sense but in ways that are complex and hard to put a finger on. You may have come across the term 'Scouse not English on football banners and related it to our accent and artful slang but it runs much deeper than this.

Unlike anywhere else in the country, it is natural for many football mad kids here to grow up not supporting England. The majority watch from a neutral perspective. Give supporters here a choice of doing the double over the other half across Stanley Park and they would bite your hand off; it is what matters.

Liverpool is not bitter towards England but simultaneously is not in its pocket and in hindsight has little to do with it. The people could probably tell you more about Ireland, Amsterdam and New York in comparison to Manchester, Birmingham and London. The Scouse accent speaks for itself and is one of the world's most unique. Pace, strength and distinction give it identity. However, you will pick up on subtle differences in dialect depending on what end of the river you visit; certain parts speak harsher and others quicker with a softer tone though the character remains the same.

Immigrants and tourists are often taken aback and returning emigrants also need to collect themselves for a brief moment to adjust, due to the lingo that is continually shifting, typical of a city on the edge of big water.

The accent contains traces of our international brothers over in Dublin, another western port city on the edge of the Ocean overlooking our transatlantic cousins of New York on the far horizon, places also noted for sharp speech, movement and culture. Liverpool, as one of the great port cities has always shared with the world the Atlantic Ocean. The past continually cracks open into the present here before it drifts away again on the tide.

The City is 'Another Place', something perfectly portrayed by our 'Iron Men' on Crosby Beach in Liverpool 23. My project is to showcase all the postcodes that make up Liverpool as a whole and how they correlate to this bigger picture. The present book will focus on images and short poems on the central areas of L1, L2 and L3 that complete the core of the City but the wider project hopes to extend from Liverpool 3 to Thirty Eight.

L1

L1 is a place of movement and the core of the city center, bordering L2, L3 and L8. It is the biggest and busiest part of central Liverpool, hosting two main train stations and Liverpool ONE, the largest open air shopping center in Britain. It contains the majority of the city's landmarks, representing both world wars, historic buildings and a tower that lights up our skyline. The hottest meeting spot in town, the area has up to a dozen main streets running through it, thriving off arrays of cafes, restaurants and pubs, all with characters of their own. A large part of the city's night life also lies here in a tight collection of streets opposite the bombed-out church. Concert Square and Seal Street alone provide an added significance to the label 'party city'. Continents worldwide are represented here. Chinatown, the Chinese quarter of the city, is easily identified by the great gate, through which lies the oldest Chinese community in Europe. Pitt Street was an emigration and immigration point for half the world, for Africa, the Indies and the United States. The Hispanic community are a much more recent feature. Spanish can be heard daily around Bold Street, Williamson Square and Mount Pleasant. Skate parks, sit off points and constant street art paint a picture of the edginess in L1, topped off by a backstreet yellow boxing gym. The end of L1 sees the Eleanor Rigby statue. Fittingly alone without a sense of place and isolated, it conveys a sense of loneliness with so much movement going on around it.

L1 Contents

St. Luke's Bombed out Church

Unique and edgy,
Displaying unspoiled skin of light brown,
It's steps frequented in the early hours of weekends,
Following a boss night on the town.
The home of student's, tourists and drinkers,
Without the normality of a roof on,
The last bombed out sight in Liverpool,
Surviving the Blitz in 1941.
The gardens of green, stretching around the outside,
The two soldiers and the ball,
Representing a Christmas Day peace pact,
Both were happy to abide.
Soldiers play with the ball, history injected into the city's core,
Having been leant a hand,
The church maintains its symbolic character,
No more war.

©Paddy Walley-Hammett

Lime Street

Brasses, seedy kids,
Those shady parts of town,
Drink, needles, brown,
A reputation that warrants a frown.
But here's a stat, active since the 1830s,
Victorian middle class to grafters and workers
The oldest grand terminus worldwide,
Liverpool on the map.

©Paddy Wailey-Hammett

Empire and The Playhouse

Two main theatres, not just L1, but Liverpool
The Playhouse and Empire, both crown jewels
Many a great, without a doubt,
Size and age make these stand out.
Britain's oldest and largest two tier,
One Night in Istanbul, a Sea of cheer!

Paddy Wailey-Hammett

6

Wellington's Column

The Duke of Wellington, 132 feet high,
The cock of the statues, the man in the sky.
The scourge of Napoleon, he looks on towards the Odeon.
The man of green, but not of the sea,
The strategist supreme, patience was key.

©Paddy Wailey-Hammett

Lewis's Statue

Accent exceedingly rare, statue exceedingly bare,
Dickie Lewis, he`s known,
in my Liverpool home.
Prometheus, Liverpool`s resurgent,
Atlantic Ocean themed,
rising ships and merchants.

©Paddy Wailey-Hammett

St. George's Hall

Reminiscent of a coliseum in ancient Rome,
Guarded by general and lions,
Graced by Victorian royalty,
Tributes set, in black and marble stone,
To scouse soldiers, battlers of the great war,
Who did not make it home
The building,
Classic, cultural,
Part of Liverpool's world heritage site,
The great plateau,
Hosting the city's annual festive market,
Song, drink and food,
Mass meetings give it extra bite,
Seven wonders stand alone.

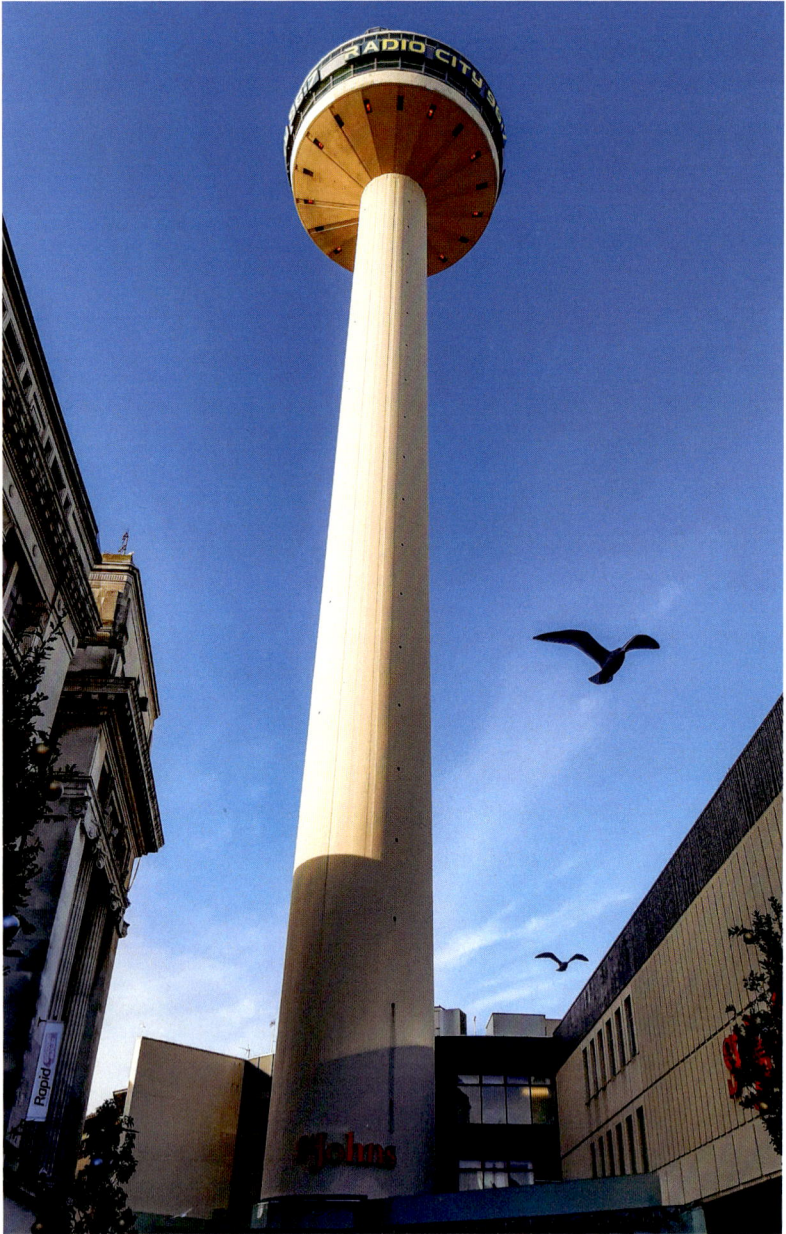

St. John's Beacon

Towering. Standing over 450 feet,
Gazing over the city and across the Mersey,
Let's onto our neighbour's on the Wirral,
Then expands into a squint,
Green and silver mountains of North Wales.
The eye of the city, but the ear of the street,
Home to Radio City,
Music, news and the banter of kids ringing in,
Having off arl Pete!

©Paddy Wailey-Hammett

The Bluecoat

1716, School Lane and Hannover Street,
The Bluey in between,
Works from Picasso and Van Gogh,
Outside of London, unseen.
Now, gourmet food, garden of green.
Weathering both wars,
The appearance of Yoko gains applause,
Modern artists, rebellion extinctioners,
Expression like expresso pours.
Rooney, Biggs and Clarke,
Quirky talent through turquoise doors.
The Bluecoat, pristine.

©Paddy Wailey Hammett

John Moores

Brings betting to the football world,
1923 almost unheard.
With Cecil's help, the brother to the right,
The dream blew up like dynamite.
Everton chairman, 1960,
Sacking great Carey in '61,
both, in a taxi, time to drive on.
He appoints Catterick, 3 cups won, a top pick.
Forever in Everton's history,
His help of Shankly seemed a mystery.
The scot's vision he saw,
Through England and Europe, they tore.
Liverpool's John Moores, a title fully earned.

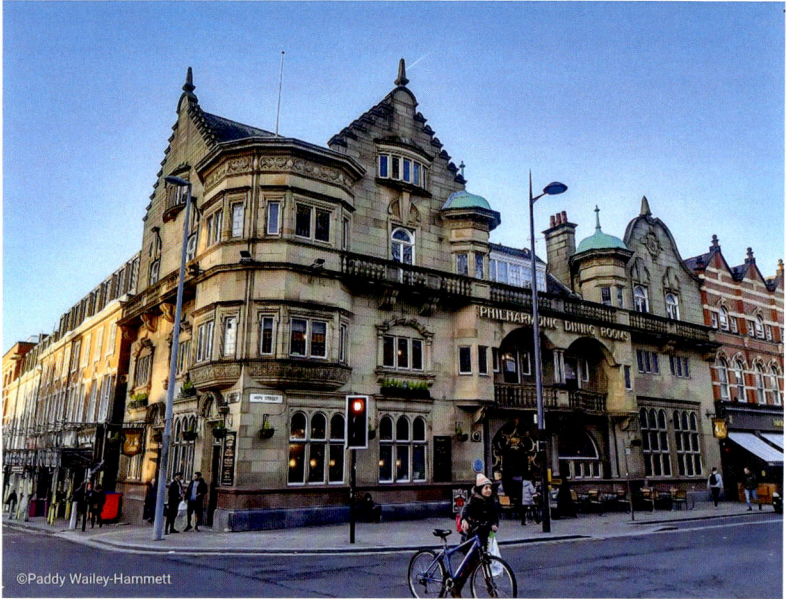
©Paddy Wailey-Hammett

18

The Philharmonic

Gold presence, articulate gem,
Locals to royal gentlemen.
Uncommon, Victorian castle,
Dogs allowed no hassle.
Spectacle, a pub cathedral,
Grade 2'sss pretty feeble,
There's Hope, however Hardman,
2020, are you a fan.
Grade 1, toilets too,
Rose marble, cameras queue.

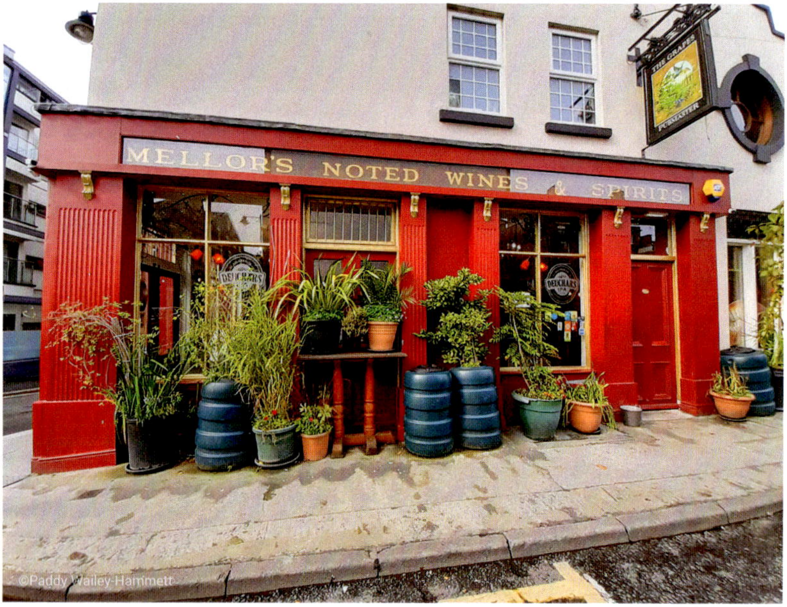
MELLOR'S NOTED WINES & SPIRITS
©Paddy Wailey-Hammett

The Grapes

Roscoe Rainforest, Famous Grapes,
Array of plants, different shapes.
Setting, the greenest,
Metaphorically, nowhere near it,
Old and new school mix,
Sunday Jazz, OJ Rum to sip.
Bright red, on the corner,
LCC she borders.

Great George's Park

Square of green,
Walled one side,
Progressively higher,
Anglican roots hide,
A presence never denied,
Blurry Great George's Road,
Endless red barrier,
Graffiti, erodes,
Syringes, cans,
Tents on the inside,
Promises of change,
Council lies.
Barricade of trees, conspicuous hedge
Tight community at the edge,
Groups of lads,
Converse, music
Moody adobe,
"Ay who's tunes it?"
Urban art, mix of sites,
Great George's Park, Skaters paradise.

Chinatown

2000, new millennium,
Chinese New Year, traditional fun.
China's arch, crowds gather, dragons march,
200, 12 pregnant mothers,
Largest outside China, bar one other.
Drawing consonants from far away continents.
Liverpool, 'Frisco and Shanghai,
Scouse to duck and rye.
Europe's oldest Chinese community,
Born from the sea.
Nelson Street, Chinese Quarter,
Zhongguo nu er, China's Daughter.

The Language House

The people, warm, sweet as Cadiz
The accent, a song, fast and strong
Shades of green, like the Irish Sea.
42 Whitechapel, language flows like wine
O Bandera Colores of Scouse Spanish ties
Regresando, The Larrinaga Line.
Colloquial style, English with a twist
Suave Francais, stressed by natives,
Cosmopolitan, learning from wider shores,
Speech of the streets on floor 3
La Escuela Mejor, Gracias a ti!

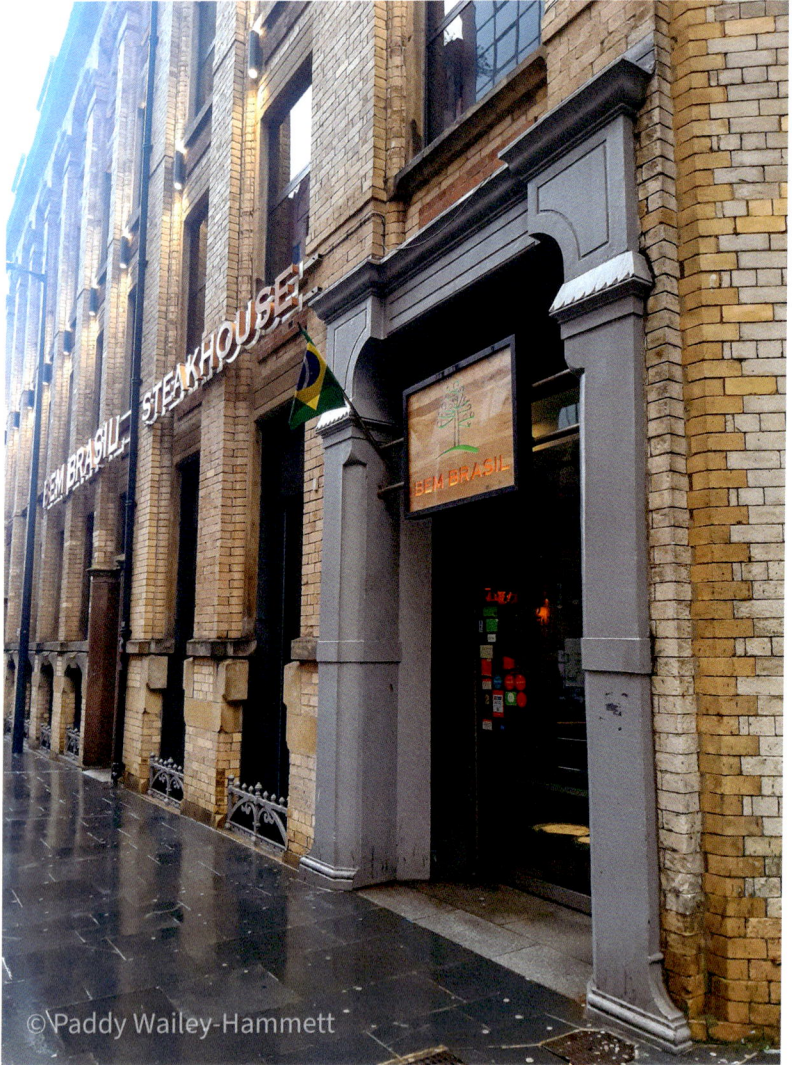

28

Bem Brazil

Viva Brasil, a momentous drop,
Flying the flag, green of the crop
Heaven for footballers, taste of back home
Senor Bobby to Phillipe Coutinho
Genius 9, a magician that shone,
Everton's Richarladson, Brazil's #1
Sumptuous buffet, all you can eat,
Portuguese wine, juiciest meat
Cafe Bossa Nova, music from the beach
Bem Brasil, Flaming Hot!

©Paddy Wailey-Hammett

La Parilla

La Parilla, spicy Mexican heat,
Drops of culture splash onto Bold Street,
Vibrant man, guitar, sings to the beat,
Huge sombrero, dancing, mariachi on repeat!
Grinning, waving, he's a case,
Street art adjoining, a smile on your face!
Sol, Bebidas, Un Poco de Gracia,
Mexico, Liverpool, both in one place.

©Paddy Walley-Hammett

Una Mujer de Cuba

Alma de Cuba, Latin vibe,
Arte bonito, hard to describe,
Pello, Liverpool red,
Sobre, Cuban blue,
Rival colours close spread.
Cuello, gold gleams,
Fresh water stone, emerald green.
Moreno skin, vestido blanco,
Contraste, white as snow.
Contenta, sonrisa enorma,
Una Grande Cubana, Si Senora!

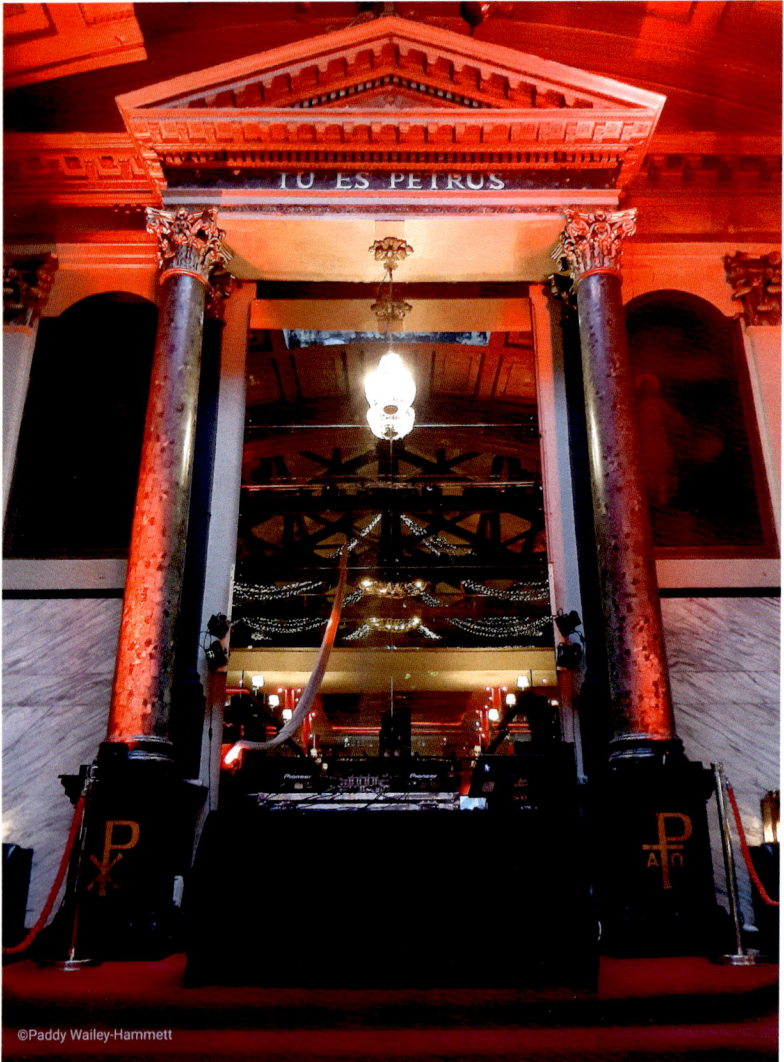

©Paddy Wailey-Hammett

Alma de Cuba

By the old Beechy of the '70s
Staggering, after plenty
Weekend in Paradise,
Finishing righteously
St. Peter's, you enter quietly,
Nowadays, Hispanic Club
Balanced swagger, much love
Altar de Alma, hardly changed,
Tu es Petrus, Holy name
Buen musica, Reggeton
Todas Felices, a spirit not gone!

Heebie Jeebies

Unchanging Heebies
Studenty and Indie
No agro, cool girls
Best place to be.
Vigorous dancefloor, pressed jeans
Cordial yard to light up and breathe.
Menthols, mixers, the ambiance sweet
Hell of a Night,
You won't forget the ones you meet.
Sole sections, downstairs parties
Converse is great but bring ID!

Concert Square

Festival square
Boxed by Fleet and Wood
Session goers lair
Wavy Port City let down your hair.
Woody's, a karaoke bar none
Pop World, jack the lad's having fun,
Evvi to halls, student dorms
Curtains to sunlight calls
MCooleys, shiny pool rooms
Live Reds and Blues, UFC nights,
Wired to stools,
Levels, 3 floors with LED walls
DJs from overseas, messiest tours
Pocket of Night life
Sounds of the 'Pool they share,
Party City, begrudgers beware.

©Paddy Wailey-Hammett

The Baltic Fleet

White ship, dark sails,
Cabin windows, many tales.
Conspicuous, sailors dock road,
Town and L8 enclosed.
Wood from Baltic, the Russian fleet,
Named in a heartbeat.
Famous lock downs, every day,
Once in, you have to stay,
'60s dockers, Wednesday lunchtimes,
Crowded with smoke, in it's prime.
The Baltic, cracking ale!

Eleanor Rigby

Rock n Roll, leather jacket
Music central, let's av it!
Bars bouncing,
Come Together, racket!
Lennon, ecstasy, magic
Worship, Beatles have it!
Stanley Street? Sack it,
What's there to see?
Deserted Eleanor Rigby
Small bench, so wide
Not a soul by her side
Buckets She's cried,
Terrible social divide,
Lord knows She's tried.
Tragic
Perfect portrayal,
McCartney's classic.

© Paddy Wailey-Hammett

St John's Gardens

Back of St. George's, the hall spreading wide,
Having the back of its treeless brother, the north side.
Pavement, clean. Cross benches, patches of green,
Flower beds; red, yellow, and orange,
Most delicate the town has seen, workers pass by
A scran unfolded, a cigarette rolled, a plane in the sky,
For that moment, a dream.
Seven monuments, the garden's pride.
Rathbone, founder of the district nursing movement,
His bronze pedestal a place for the NHS,
Gladstone, the Liverpudlian Prime Minister,
First and last, we have had to address.
Parchment, truth and justice the words say,
Justice for the car accidents of today,
A spare thought, a tribute to bitter pain,
Lester, founder of children's charities in Liverpool,
Paving the way,
Nugent, ensuring one less ragged kid is led astray.
Service of the King's regiment, South Africa, Boer War,
A soldier, shot, dying on the floor,
Go out quietly, he cannot.
"Oh, I am a Liverpudlian, I come from the Spion Kop,
I like to sing, I like to shout, I go there quite a lot!"
Britannia soldiers, guns, a boy on the drums,
Anfield, rocking and roaring, screaming top of her
lungs, *Poor Scouser Tommy*, they sing and cry.

The Egyptian Wizard

The Bohemian

©Paddy Walley-Hammett

Lennon and the Crown of Thorns

©Paddy Wailey Hammett

L2

L2 is the bottom end of town, past L1 and bordering L3 in the direction of the river.

The original town centre, it is made up of five main streets, three of which belong to the original seven in Liverpool, Castle Street, Water Street and Tithebarn Street. A prominent pocket, this zone bears treasures that are celebrated as the first of their kind on a worldwide scale. The raucous Matthew Street and Oriel Chambers are fine examples.

Eye catching pubs and train stations are also a continual theme, contributing heavily to the art and history of the area. Derby Square marks the start of the district, containing the robust Queen Victoria monument as well as Liverpool Crown Court, where many deep and dark trials have been held. Formerly known for its banking, Castle Street is now described as a food mecca, ranging from Italian plates and pizzas to gin dispensaries and European style cafes. The new modern, upmarket style is popular amongst footballers, wags and bent property magnates.

Past the wave of establishments stands the Georgian Town Hall, the equivalent of any of the great buildings of Britain. Wherever Liverpool is spoken about, The Beatles spring to mind. Nowhere else is this more relevant than Matthew Street, the music quarter of the city, where the 'Fab Four' are celebrated every day and by an annual festival.

Vibrant pubs set a welcoming presence on Tithebarn street, the rainbow- coloured Kitty's symbolizing its energy and free spirit. A stone throw away is Shenanigans, a modern pub that is flying the flag for the Liverpool Irish, something that is summed up perfectly by its cinematic street art on the car park wall.

Guarding Liverpool John Moores is the Superlambanana, a bright yellow, unorthodox creature that stands over 17 feet, marking the huge success of our 2008 capital of culture.

Hackins Hey, an ancient alleyway that runs off Tithebarn street is reminiscent to Whitechapel and also belongs to the Georgian era. The Hey is home to Liverpool's first ever pub, Ye Hole in Ye Wall and many a Shanghaied sailor. Water Street accommodates St. Mary's, The Sailors Church, home to 'Homeless Jesus', a sculpture that paints a thousand words, it is the last stop in L2, before joining the Pier Head where millions have arrived at the city by water.

L2 Contents

©Paddy Wailey-Hammett

Liverpool Crown Court

Derby Square, Liverpool Crown Court
Months to stretches, don't get caught,
Notorious, some heavy cases
Mercer, Warren,
The many faces
Christmas tree, colour of grass
Plod vehicles, strangers pass,
Imposing, what it appears
Sweating, prison fears
Ruthless, the highest tier
Kid; don't come here!

58

Victoria

Through the wire, she stood,
Catastrophic bombs, untouched
Queen of an empire, based on slavery,
The blithe State shames me.
Cotton, the darkest symbol
Centuries of pain, criminal
Liverpool's distant past
White bales on Exchange flags
Her initial visit, sad
Victoria, erected by a cotton man,
England's patriotism, crap.

Superlambanana

Superlambanana, humour
Liverpool unorthodox, never truer
Inspired by movement, port trade,
Meat and fruit, common as waves.
08, Capital of Culture
125 more vivid sculptures
Colossal.
Tithebarn Street's dinosaur
22 years on,
Without a flaw!

© Paddy Wailey-Hammett

© Paddy Wailey-Hammett

James Street Platform 2

James Street, Platform 2
A snidey entrance, known to few,
Closed to the public, suspicious stews,
Matrix skies, velvet and pink
Mysterious, script relived,
Enigmatic graffiti, interpretation unknown
Urban brimmed, a Bronx style zone
Brass plaques, the 7 streets
Original Town, The Welsh Fleet
Worth a risk to view!

© Paddy Walley-Hammett

Railway Exchange

The stony station, railway now changed,
Streaming honey, lonely in the rain
Hanging faces, seen with a strain
Fine print letters, neatly engraved
Farewell Exchange,
We'll see you again.

©Paddy Wailey-Hammett

The Town Hall

Castle Street, Town Hall
Georgian class, embedded walls
Vintage block, can't ignore,
One of few, will never fall,
The Mayor's Kennel they call,
Unparalleled, best of all.

© Paddy Wailey-Hammett

Oriel Chambers

Iron framework, glass curtain wall
Prestigious, palace of the North
The world's first, inspiring New York.
A US messenger, Wells Fargo
To the skyscrapers of Chicago
Oriel Chambers, Water Street's draw.

Ye Hole in Ye Wall

Ye Hole, antique tongue
1726, the journey begun,
Blazing fire, brass, wood on wall
True old school, cellar first floor
However, these bricks bear more,
Tales of ghosts and gore
The Spanish Sailor,
Blanked The King's Shilling
Heartlessly stabbed, a brutal killing
Chilling, never the same
Whispers say his presence remains,
But no need to fear,
Six cask ales, top beer
Proper pub, visit's a must.

Shenanigans

Number 77, square and tall
Charismatic, loved by all,
Bright layers, positive vibes
Irish green, a hint of lime
Sun and moon, balanced energy
Drinks splurging,
Guinness, Hennessy
Four leaf clover, precious sites
Red haired beauty, on your bikes
Dublin and Liverpool,
Two gripping hands,
The Irish Capital,
Forever our brand
Service in Lockdown,
Heroically done,
Shenanigans, Always Welcome.

Matthew Street

Legendary Matthew Street,
L2's heartbeat
Best ever band, their old boozers
To visit, everyone chooses
Cool statues, abstract murals
Tourist Central, never dull,
Choc a bloc, millions each year
Nest of Beatles, distinctly clear
Every song, volume off chart
4 lads, never apart
The Cavern Quarter,
Never sleeps.

Yellow Submarine

'68 Cartoon, masterpiece
An unusual spectator street
Rainbow of colour, psychedelic
Cheerful, hippies relish
Deep, dream and reality
Trippy as can be,
Bitter blues, meanies
Strawberry Fields, dreamy
Yellow Sub, the sea of time
Paradise, *Lucy in the Sky*
Characters, a wall with weed,
Landmark, best we've seen!

Cilla Black

Loved by The Beatles, a Liverpool affair
Her first start,
Anyone Who Had a Heart
64, topped the Chart,
Her stage, the seething club
Early days, lit up,
Shiny statue,
The Cavern's flair.

John Lennon

Lennon, not their greatest musician
Peace, laughter and wisdom,
Millions miss him,
Genius writer, none shone brighter,
On the mic, smashing it,
Gigs going, full kit,
Imagine, words so true,
All you need is love, few argue,
John, praise we give him.

©Paddy Walley-Hammett

The Sailors Church

Sailors church, spire bearing North,
Maritime resonance, first sight they saw,
Coming upriver Our Lady or St. Nick's
Numerous names, take your pick,
A place of acceptance, a parish
12th century, ancient status.

©Paddy Wailey-Hammett

84

Homeless Jesus

Jesus was a sailor,
When he walked upon the river
Cohen's *Suzanne*, a thriller
Only drowning men could see him,
Eternal freedom.
A maritime city, blessed,
The church of his mother, he rests,
A visual translation, The Bible
A message to his disciples
Turning from someone in need,
Is the same as turning from him,
Help the homeless,
always give.

L3

L3 is a diverse place of movement with the river at its heart. It is the most widespread downtown postcode, dipping into districts outside of the Centre, the fast- flowing tide being the perfect metaphor. The Pier Head catches the eye of many ferries and cruise ships across the Mersey, greeted by families heading out to Seacombe or New York, the near and local to the far horizon. The Birkenhead tunnel typifies the area as a significant connection to the Wirral peninsula. The city's biggest tourist attractions lie in Liverpool 3 and are visited daily by faces from every part of the world, hence our nickname of 'The World in One City'. We are very proud of the Beatles and the waterfront is one of the Fab Four's many Liverpool homes, a shout away from their idol Billy Fury, a worker, a trendsetter and nature lover in his element so close to the river and along from 'The Birds'. The Liver Birds portray Liverpool as a maritime city guiding seamen on ships and are ever present on the chests of both Liverpool F C and Liverpool Schoolboys. Movement and passage between land and water is common in major port cities and something that is captured by Liverpool's central docks. The docks are of great importance and are recognised for their impact on cultures worldwide. The Salthouse Dock is the city's oldest and carries a level of notoriety due to its involvement in the slave trade, having dispatched many a ship destined for Africa and The West Indies. The present-day dock is full of life and boasts a unique marine biodiversity; seaweed and Korean barnacles give it an ocean presence. The Albert Dock is now a national symbol and the cities most renowned, appearing in many documentaries on both a regional and national scale. The Dock contains the Tate Gallery and Jesse Hartley's old brick warehouses that stand serene and reflect calmly on clear water to provide an art effect of their own. The Canning is known for its lock gates which until recently were made from Canada green wood, the toughest in the world. Hundreds of personalised love locks and lockets hang beautifully off metal chains that surround the dock walls. The locks act as an outlet to the river and represents Movement and a passageway to the world. The Maritime Museum is also here, the most popular attraction amongst visitors in Liverpool. Passed the Pier Head and up the Dock Road is a very different set of docks. Entering Vauxhall, this area has an industrial setting and is closer to the Liverpool of old. The Vauxhall Bridge is the marker for the North end docks and the border between L3 and L5. To the right of the bridge, continuing north is the Stanley dock, finely boxed in between the historic Spirit, Tea and Tobacco warehouses and again with a direct opening to the Mersey. At its mouth the six faced Salisbury Clock is the only one of its kind left in the world. Detailed views of the Wirral are enjoyed from here. Looking inwards, the Stanley locks mark the beginning of the Liverpool to Leeds Canal. Beside it, Vauxhall's Eldonian Village, on the site of the old sugar refinery, is now a cooperative association and has the feel of a tight knit local community. The estate is just west of Scotland Road, regarded by residents as the heart of the North end. Eldon Grove, a little off Eldonian Way is its most distinctive pocket. The Gothic Church, bordered by a large patch of conspicuous moss, gravel and brick is a dream for any modern style photographer. The Grove's listed buildings, derelict and of timber frame are a precious asset. Liverpool is holy in more ways than one. You would be hard pressed to find a district that is without multiple places of worship, whether that be Catholic, Protestant, Jewish or Muslim. The Metropolitan, locally known as 'Paddy's Wigwam' is the more modern of our two Cathedrals and arguably our most renowned building of the modern era. The memorial garden of the Holy Cross, also Catholic, is a lot more discreet and one of the city's true hidden gems. Located on Standish Street, the garden represents a fascinating history of Liverpool's often fiery relationships between, Catholics and Protestants, happily now a thing of the past. The student quarter of the city runs along the east of the district away from the river and borders Edge Hill. Street names and pubs are named after prestigious institutions that exist here and reflect the importance of education, Science and research. The School of Tropical Medicine places the highest emphasis on Sub Saharan research and 200 million has been invested from overseas organisations to assist the development of effective vaccinations in the battle against Covid. North of the University, on London Road is the Royal Liverpool University Hospital, bang in the middle of both the street and a crisis, having lost so many during the pandemic. Liverpool is a place of humour and warmth but it is also very much a fighting city, embedded over centuries. Mixed Martial Arts has taken the city by storm in the last decade and has proven just as popular as football for many of the younger generation. Next GEN, on Kempton Street, is Liverpool's first ever mixed martial arts school, introduced by Paul Rimmer, who is regarded by many as one of the top trainers in the UK. Since opening its doors, the gym has seen the birth and growth of many top fighters, competing in professional organisations such as Bellator, Cage Warriors and the pinnacle, the UFC itself. The gym has been an excellent ambassador for the city and has helped assist individuals from every walk of life in the form of self- defence, discipline, fitness and mental health. The gym has a fighting style theme of impressive and creative graffiti, something common to the surrounding streets. Passed Low Hill, L3 once again becomes the North end and enters the start of Everton. East of the river; the park is the cut- off point to L5. Hope University is the initial opening of Everton and neighbours eminent College Streets. Salisbury Street is one of the city's most spirited and is home to the church of Saint Francis Xavier and Salisbury ABC, which is named after it. The Solly holds a unique story of moving three times without leaving the Street, the church being a former stop. It has a classic old school feel about it but with the balance of modern equipment and knowledge. The ABC is of great success and boasts an unbelievable resume' of accomplishments, produced by an outstanding pool of fighters and trainers from past to present. However, the gym is much more than silverware and acts as a great gate post for the community, a rewarding environment of hard graft and fun. The Solly is forever raising funds for food banks across the district. The Street is the last outpost and defines L3 as a place of movement, purpose, history and fight. Liverpool is a very passionate City.

L3 Contents

Abercromby Square

Oxford Street North,
The Cambridge South,
History and Art, Liverpool throughout
Abercromby Square, gardens at the heart
University green, *The Peoples Park*
Multitudes of shoes, peaceful,
Plane trees with views,
War Gazebo, Cathedral
Thanks Commander Ralph.

© Paddy Wailey-Hammett

94

Victorian Building

1887, Victoriae Reginae
Signature building, pinnacle of the city
Red brick, common as Hall Road
Chocolate Ruaban, Welsh stone
Razor spikes, hogwarts hats
L shaped tower, a student habitat
Gold four faced clock,
Brownlow Hill, 79 bus- stop,
L69... taking the Mickey?

© Paddy Wailey-Hammett

University of Liverpool

Communal, public,
Trademark red brick, another civic
Part of the original six
Widespread, 100 subjects
Lengua mezclada, mixing and text,
Cosmopolitan, ahead of its time,
Xian Jualang, establishments in China!
Founded on shipping rates,
Watertight base
The full package,
Soul and wit of *'This Place'*
Live, More and Hope,
Words of promise.

© Paddy Wailey-Hammett

Royal Hospital

Covid zone, fear grows,
Conspiracists, spitting and twitching,
Real talk, far from those doors
Claps on the Avenue, murals on walls
The Mystery Streets, our full support
Worldwide virus, sidelong in flight
Lives on the line, a foe in disguise,
Tories for leave, fear anything free
Money for land, not PPE
So, we stress, bless the NHS,
To all those fallen, God rest.
The Royal, Home to Heroes.

To the Glory of God & to the Memory of the Men of Holy Cross C.Y.M.S. who fell in the World War
1914 — 1918
1939 — 1945

© Paddy Wailey-Hammett

Holy Cross

Latent landmark, remote light
A Saint's garden, clear of eyes
North end of the centre, hidden gem
Commemorating fallen men
Catholic service, 1909
Causing stern, times of divide
Netherfield Road, Blue L5
Once strong Orange, Protestants thrived,
Riots,
Bottles and fires,
1911 the city unites,
Soldiers of the Holy Cross, Goodnight.

102

Metropolitan Cathedral

Picture painting, thorn crown
A skyline God, eyes all around
Bygone relics, Celtic cone
Stained glass saints, *You'll Never Walk Alone*
Trio of crosses, Passion of Christ
Luminous tent, a light for the night
Metropolitan Cathedral, Liverpool Renowned.

© Paddy Wailey-Hammett

Art Deco

Art Deco,
Draining air from below
Desert stream, cars flow
Engine house, tunnelled mouth
Birkenhead bound, watered Scouse,
Choppy Mersey, a constant toast.

Liverpool's Wheel

Liverpool, a whirling wheel
Movement and banter, coastal appeal
River Thames, Cockney East End,
Same fast pace, bursting edge,
Drink and dance, Polish Gdansk,
Eastern Toon, tidal cities,
Always shifting,
Raging and roaring, belligerent ports
Manila's Rivers, Europe's New York
We say how we feel.

Liver Birds

Crested Cormorants, mythical beasts
Latching liver seaweed, content as can be,
Top of the clocks, on the city's arm,
Free.
One observes the land,
The other watches the sea,
Expecting old seamen, to bring prosperity,
Anfield red, river green.
Tatted on arms and calves,
The breast of LFC
Birds that will never cheat.

© Paddy Walley Hammett

Salthouse Dock

1753, triangular trade
Port city, born from famine and slaves,
The southern dock, launching sail,
West African Coast, Hammerheads and Whales
Middle passage, Indigenous Indies
Exchange Flags, nearing 1850s,
Cheshire rock salt, bold blocks
Dublin Bay, Scotland's Ness Lock
French Mediterranean, giant snails
Present in today's Bay,
Ocean seaweed, jelly stingers
Dry suits, kayaks,
Under the bridge
Abounding with boats, precisely different,
Like toys on the Atlantic
Salthouse Dock, sunshine and rain.

Albert Dock

Barques and Coasters in 1846
To WW2's Atlantic ships
Merchant cargo
Brandy, tobacco and sugar
The Great Albert, dockers lover
Alluring Tate,
Three Graces through the lock
Fiery reflections, unbroken water
Old warehouses, new shops
Royal Charter, boss fish.

© Paddy Wailey-Hammett

The Fab Four

4 kids and South Liverpool
Writing over *Penny Lane*
Whistling Dovedale, Caldies School
George, Wavertree born
Ringo from the Dingle
Mossley Hill for John and Paul
Leaders of youth, music culture worldwide
Working class lads, the Right they despise
Hard Rock and Pop, Psychedelic Blues
Mops on their heads, shining black shoes,
Multi coloured faces, tens of races
Come Together, places, traces,
Arnold Grove, Childwall's Abbey Road
A World in One City, The Beatles we owe,
Life happens to everyone,
Through their songs they live on.

©Paddy Wailey-Hammett

Billy Fury

Ronald Wycherley, South end's Streets
Cousin of Allan,
The world at his feet
His Great Nephew, a good friend of mine
Smoke and a pint, *'Halfway to Paradise'*
Good looks, crisp wit
Larger than life, shades of Elvis
Initial script, face of the ships
Slick quiff blowing in the wind,
Last stop, honest docker
Leaving the river adrift,
When time came knocking
Silver Beatles,
Lennon and the lads
'Maybe Tomorrow'
We'll get his autograph!'
Bird watcher, wildlife lover
Gulls and the water, no place other
Billy Fury, first on the scene.

© Paddy Wailey-Hammett

Stanley Dock

Sky blue, sloping trees,
Faint reflections, clear water
Rocks, keys
Meeting eyes beneath
Looping tunnel, the Aintree train
Fishermen, urban paint
Lending soul to this flowing terrain
Tobacco Warehouse, The Vauxhall Bridge
Shuddered by trucks, built like ships,
Shivering river, strong and loyal
Dazzling blue, Big Joe Royal
Salisbury Clock, black and white eyed,
Worn as The Wirral is wide
Stanley Dock, Industrial L3.

© Paddy Wailey-Hammett

Eldonian Village

Eldonian Village,
Stone's throw to the unknown
Vauxhall, unwithdrawn
Scotty channel, North end's jaw
Eldon Grove, lovely landmarks
Unroofed and unused, beautifully abandoned
De la Salette across
Catalunya Quarter
Imagination, creation
Hypnotic tour
Big Liverpool, a world within it.

© Paddy Wailey-Hammett

© Paddy Wailey-Hammett

The Solly

1974, The Salisbury
Three times moved, loyal to the Street,
Prominent, Town's ABC
Many a name
Derry Matthews to Pricey
Classic amateur, giving help and direction,
ABAs, Schoolboy Champions
Success without question
Rising stars, future faces on the wall
Tucker to Hyland, The Flyweight Southpaw
Paul Eddy, steering the ship,
Alan Lynch, start to finish,
The Solly, blue she bleeds.

© Paddy Wailey-Hammsteld

Next Gen MMA

Brazilian Ju Jitsu, physical chess
world class grapplers, UK's best
Wrestling, striking, rolling on mats,
All levels welcome, white belt to black
Next Gen of winners,
Cage Warriors Belts, three divisions
Chris Fishgold, no fear
Paddy the Baddy, pioneer
26 finishes, submission killers
Meatball Molly, her hand raised,
A female Scouser, the biggest stage
Dan Hot Chocolate, swiftest boxer
UFC cemented, plenty to offer,
Head Coach, Paul Rimmer
Martial Artist, Community Figure
Liverpool's first school, spirits none bigger.

Soul Train

126

Women and Football

©Paddy Wailey-Hammett

A Passage to The World